HOW TO EVALUATE SERMONS

HOW TO
EVALUATE
SERMONS

Joel R. Beeke

PUBLISHING WITH A MISSION

EP BOOKS
Faverdale North
Darlington, DL3 0PH, England

web: http://www.epbooks.org
e-mail: sales@epbooks.org

First published 2012

British Library Cataloguing in Publication Data available

ISBN-13: 978-0-85234-778-2
ISBN-10: 0-85234-778-2

Unless otherwise indicated, all Scripture quotations are from the Holy Bible, Authorized (King James) Version.

Printed and bound in the UK.

CONTENTS

Who then is Paul, and who is Apollos, but ministers by whom ye believed, even as the Lord gave to every man? I have planted, Apollos watered; but God gave the increase. So then neither is he that planteth any thing, neither he that watereth; but God that giveth the increase. Now he that planteth and he that watereth are one: and every man shall receive his own reward according to his own labour. For we are labourers together with God: ye are God's husbandry, ye are God's building. According to the grace of God which is given unto me, as a wise masterbuilder, I have laid the foundation, and another buildeth thereon. But let every man take heed how he buildeth thereupon. For other foundation can no man lay than that is laid, which is Jesus Christ. Now if any man build upon this foundation gold, silver, precious stones, wood, hay, stubble; every man's work shall be made manifest: for the day shall declare it, because it shall be revealed by fire; and the fire shall try every man's work of what sort it is. If any man's work abide which he hath built thereupon, he shall receive a reward. If any man's work shall be burned, he shall suffer loss: but he himself shall be saved; yet so as by fire

(1 Corinthians 3:5–15).

In the 2010 Winter Olympics, speed-skater Sven Kramer was poised to win a second gold medal. He pressed forward in the last eight of twenty-five laps in the gruelling 10,000 metre race. He had a six-second lead on the men behind him, and victory seemed sure. But then Kramer's coach shouted: 'Inner lane!' Kramer hesitated, then changed lanes, finishing the race for what he believed was a sure win.

His race earned him nothing, as Olympic officials ruled that Kramer's cross into the wrong lane disqualified him from the race. The loss was far worse for his coach. 'This is the worst moment of my career,' he said.[1] What a tragedy for those highly skilled men after years of training!

It is far worse for a servant of the Lord to cross the boundaries of his calling, thereby losing some of the heavenly reward that might have been his. The Bible reminds us that an athlete does not receive the victor's crown unless he competes according to the rules (2 Tim. 2:5). This tragedy is not limited to scandalous falls and apostasies that bring open shame to ministers of the gospel. It is also evident in the quiet lane changes by which godly preachers of the Word operate outside their Lord's will. These errors do not disqualify a man's pastoral ministry, but they do compromise his calling and will ultimately cost him some reward.

As preachers, we are like spiritual athletes who need to keep growing and developing our skills.

We also function as spiritual coaches to Christ's church. Our sermons seriously affect those under our care; our responsibility is great. It is especially frightening for a preacher to press forward with energy and satisfaction, realizing how he erred only after reaching the finish line.

We must regularly evaluate our preaching to know if we are growing as preachers. Charles Spurgeon (1834–1892) said to his ministerial students, 'I give you the motto, "Go forward." Go forward in personal attainments, forward in gifts and in grace, forward in fitness for the work, and forward in conformity to the image of Jesus.' He went on to say, 'If there be any brother here who thinks he can preach as well as he should, I would advise him to leave off altogether.'[2]

How do you evaluate yourself as a preacher? A preacher's view of his own messages can be an emotional roller-coaster ride driven by his moods and the responses of the congregation. We dare not evaluate ourselves by measurable results such as increased attendance or new members joining the church, for people often flock to false teachers like flies to manure. Nor can we gauge our effectiveness by a brother who shoots out of a worship service like a bullet out of a rifle, or a woman who gets misty-eyed and emotional in shaking our hand after a sermon. For all we know, the brother was suddenly taken ill, and the sister recently received bad news about a distant relative. Neither response necessarily has anything to do with our preaching. My father was once so moved by a child's intense listening that he questioned her about what she found so important. She responded: 'I was trying to figure out if you had shaved this morning.'

This does not mean we should plough forward without reflection, however. We need standards for self-evaluation. Our habitual standard should be *to evaluate our preaching as a servant anticipating our Master's evaluation.* In 1 Corinthians 1, the apostle Paul addresses the issue of division within the church, specifically in people's preference for one teacher over another, such as Paul or Apollos or Peter (1 Cor. 1:10–12). Chapter 3 opens with Paul accusing the Corinthians of petty, childish bickering. He says in 1 Corinthians 3:4: 'For while one saith, I am of Paul; and another, I am of Apollos; are ye not carnal?' This sets the stage for 1 Corinthians 3:5–15, in which Paul tells the church how to evaluate teachers of the Word. The text has huge implications for how pastors and Bible teachers should view their own ministry. In telling us that we must each evaluate our preaching as a servant anticipating his master's evaluation, this text suggests five questions to ask ourselves about our preaching. Each question provides both a motivation and a method for evaluating our sermons.

Did I preach as God's servant?

The apostle says in 1 Corinthians 3:5-8: 'Who then is Paul, and who is Apollos, but ministers by whom ye believed, even as the Lord gave to every man? I have planted, Apollos watered; but God gave the increase. So then neither is he that planteth any thing, neither he that watereth; but God that giveth the increase. Now he that planteth and he that watereth are one: and every man shall receive his own reward according to his own labour.'

The word *ministers* (in Greek, *diakonoi*) refers to household servants under the authority of a master or Lord (*kurios*, *cf.* Luke 12:37). No matter what their tax forms say, ministers are not self-employed. We are not independent agents free to do as we please; we are servants of the King. The Lord assigns to us our vocation and he rewards us accordingly. Though the Lord gives us different gifts, different placements, and different degrees of fruitfulness, we are one in our calling as his servants. Instead of evaluating our work by comparing it to other preachers, we should evaluate it in comparison to the Lord's commands.

We are also farmers who plant and irrigate our fields but cannot make the seeds grow. Cornfields often have signs posting what kind of seed the farmer planted, such as Pioneer, Agrigold, or DeKalb. The signs remind us that much depends upon the life within the seed, not the farmer. A thousand factors determine the yield of a crop, almost all of which God directly controls. How much more, then, are ministers dependent upon the work of God the Holy Ghost to save and sanctify people by the life-giving seed of his Word? We can do nothing by ourselves. Charles Hodge (1797–1878) said in his commentary on this text, 'Ministers are mere instruments in the hands of God. The doctrines which they preach are not their own discoveries, and the power which renders their preaching successful is not in them.'[3]

As a servant under the Lord's authority, a preacher should evaluate his sermons based upon their fidelity to Holy Scripture. 1 Corinthians 4:1 tells us that preachers are 'stewards of the mysteries of God'. You are God's delivery-man to bring his message to others; you are not the author of the message. A messenger who rushes off without first listening to his Master's words exposes himself to great shame.

So evaluate your sermons with what I will call *humble exegesis*, with the criteria of a humble servant, asking if you:

- Approached the Scripture with a willingness to be taught and corrected by God, or assumed that you already knew what the Scripture said;
- Spent enough time and energy to study that Scripture text and let God speak to you through it;
- Read the commentaries of godly and wise teachers to check your interpretation;
- Derived the main idea and points from the clear statement of a Scripture text;
- Spent time explaining what the text meant so your listeners could better understand it;
- Based applications of your sermon on the Scriptures, not just on your vision for the church;
- Preached a message that was faithful to the text's meaning in its context;
- Demonstrated to your hearers that your sermon came from God's Word instead of your own ideas, thoughts, or opinions.

Since your ministry depends on God's power, you should also evaluate your preaching in prayers of *humble dependence*. Without the Holy Spirit you are no more useful than an unplugged power saw. So ask yourself as a servant of the Saviour if you:

- Planned this series and this specific sermon, prayerfully asking God for wisdom;
- Enlisted your congregation to pray for your preaching;
- Studied the Scripture text on your knees, with fervent pleas for illumination;
- Prepared the sermon in the context of regular, private prayers for the church;
- Cried out to God prior to the worship services for the Spirit's anointing;
- Cried out to God after the services for divine application;
- Gave God all the glory for any good that resulted from your efforts.

Do you feel an urgent need for the anointing of the Holy Spirit? One of the greatest preachers of the last century, Dr D. Martyn Lloyd-Jones (1899–1981), wrote:

Do you always look for and seek this unction, this anointing before preaching? Has this been your greatest concern? ... It is God giving power, and enabling, through the Spirit, to the preacher in order that he may do this work in a manner that lifts it up beyond the efforts and endeavours of man to a position in which the preacher is being used by the Spirit and becomes a channel through which the Spirit works.[4]

You must ask yourself: 'Did I preach as God's servant?' Evaluate your sermons for any hint that you stood in the pulpit as a lord and saviour instead of a humble servant and messenger whose authority comes solely from God.

DID I PREACH TO BUILD GOD'S CHURCH?

Paul goes on to say in 1 Corinthians 3:9: 'For we are labourers together with God: ye are God's husbandry [farm], ye are God's building.' The Greek text stresses that this entire project belongs to God when it says, 'God's workers ... God's field ... and God's building.'[5] The metaphor shifts from agriculture to construction as God tells his servants to build the people of the church, which verse 16 says is 'the temple of God'.

God is the architect of his temple. He is also the general contractor and the glorious Being who inhabits this house. Ministers are labourers whom God hires to build his house, a building not made of wood, brick, stone, or steel, but of 'living stones', the people of God. 'Ye are God's building,' our text says. Therefore the construction metaphor communicates the love of our covenant God who wants to dwell in eternal intimacy with his people.

The Lord aims not only to make his home among us but also to make us his home.

The purpose of preaching, then, is not to produce a work of theological or rhetorical art abstracted from human need. It is to build up God's living and holy temple — men, women and children — in Christ. Preaching the Word is the divinely appointed means to bring God and his people together in eternal, mutual love.

J. I. Packer writes:

> *Christianity, on earth as in heaven, is … fellowship with the Father and with his Son Jesus Christ, and the preaching of God's Word in the power of God's Spirit is the activity that … brings the Father and the Son down from heaven to dwell with men.*[6]

This means your preaching must be helpful to people. So ask yourself: in preparing your sermons, did you:

- Write your sermon with an eye to your flock and their needs?
- Labour hard and long on this sermon out of love, or were you lazy?
- Organize the message to make listening easier for people?
- Begin with an introduction (either before or

after giving out your text) to engage people's minds and lead them to the main idea?

- Clearly state the main idea of the message?
- Highlight the main points so that listeners recognized them?
- State your main idea and points so succinctly that a twelve-year-old boy and a seventy-year-old woman could write them in their notes?
- Help people understand ancient culture and customs foreign to their world?
- Limit your time and content to what your hearers can profitably absorb?
- Illustrate each major point to engage their imagination and affections?
- Craft your illustrations to make them helpful for understanding and applying the gospel?
- Make specific applications throughout the sermon relevant to people's lives?
- Conclude the sermon by pressing the main idea home to listeners?
- Express the loving heart of the Father who calls prodigals home?
- Call the unsaved to repentance and faith in Christ?

Love for the congregation must also motivate us to consider the varying spirituality of our listeners. William Perkins reminds us that our people have different spiritual capacities and needs. The preacher is like a housewife preparing a meal for a family ranging from a diabetic grandfather to voracious teenagers to a toddler. You must preach law and gospel in the right proportion to a group of people with various needs. Ask yourself, did you:

- Rebuke unbelievers who are ignorant and unteachable?
- Offer basic catechetical truths to unbelievers who are ignorant but teachable?
- State the terms of the law to people with knowledge but who are not yet believers?
- Offer the gospel call and comfort of Christ to unbelievers humbled by sin?
- Explain the doctrines of grace and the rule of life to believers?
- Stress the doctrines of repentance and hope to backsliding believers?[7]

No sermon can do everything, but if your sermons consistently address only some people or certain topics, you may be neglecting the spiritual needs of a significant number of your hearers.

Nothing can replace a burning love in the heart when we actually deliver the sermon. A match cannot start a fire until it is alight. So, ask yourself, did I preach with warm love, affection and kindness to my hearers? Thomas Murphy (1823–1900) wrote: 'Preaching should be with tenderness.'[8] The wife of Jonathan Edwards said to her brother after George Whitefield (1714–1770) preached in Northampton, Massachusetts,

> *It is wonderful to see what a spell he casts over an audience by proclaiming the simplest truths of the Bible ... He speaks from a heart all aglow with love.*[9]

When evaluating your preaching, ask yourself whether you preached with a burning love for God which made you long to see his church built up on earth. God loves his church with an everlasting love. If you love God, your preaching must be full of love for God's church. If you serve God, your preaching must serve his church. Did you preach to build God's church?

Did I preach Christ as the only foundation?

Paul says in 1 Corinthians 3:10-11: 'According to the grace of God which is given unto me, as a wise master builder, I have laid the foundation, and another buildeth thereon. But let every man take heed how he buildeth thereupon. For other foundation can no man lay than that is laid, which is Jesus Christ.' Without a solid foundation, a building cannot withstand harsh winds and rain. Over time, or perhaps in a single climactic storm, it will collapse (Matt. 7:24-27). A compromised foundation will cause the building's walls to shift, crack, and ultimately to fall. Jonathan Edwards (1703–1758) experienced this when a spring thaw shifted his old church meeting house in 1737. A gallery full of people fell upon those sitting in the pews below. By God's remarkable grace, no one was killed.[10]

The context of our text makes it clear that Christ is the church's only sure foundation, so we must preach Christ crucified for the faith of his called ones (1 Cor. 1:18, 22-24). Verse 10 says that Paul laid this foundation in Corinth in his preaching.[11] Paul writes in 1 Corinthians 2:2, 5: 'For I determined not to know any thing among you, save Jesus Christ, and him crucified … that your faith should not stand in the wisdom of men, but in the power of God.' By God's sovereign will, Christ is everything to the believer: our wisdom, righteousness, sanctification and redemption (1 Cor. 1:30). Christ is not only the door into salvation; he is the entire road on which we must travel to glory.

Matthew Henry (1662–1714) wrote: 'The doctrine of our Saviour and his mediation is the principal doctrine of Christianity. It lies at the bottom, and is the foundation of all the rest. Leave out this, and you lay waste all our comforts, and leave no foundation for our hopes as sinners.'[12] Ministers must therefore ask themselves whether they are preaching Christ crucified, Christ risen, and Christ all-sufficient for his people. If you fail in this, you fail to feed people the Bread of life. Their souls will starve without Christ. So ask yourself, did I:

- Write this sermon in the confidence that Christ, in his offices of Prophet, Priest and King, has in himself the fulness of wisdom, grace and power that everyone needs?

- Write this knowing that Christ is the Bible's main character and fulfilment of its every theme?
- Connect this text to Christ so that people will be encouraged to lean on him in trust?
- Thoughtfully consider how this text points to Christ?
- Seek to display men's need for grace and Christ's full provision of grace?
- Press upon hearers their obligation to keep God's law as well as seek justification before God by faith alone in Christ alone?
- Direct people to obey by faith in the sanctifying grace of Jesus Christ?
- Explain that the gospel is both for the salvation of the lost and for the lives of the saved?
- Preach Christ not only as useful to us but as gloriously beautiful and worthy of our worship?
- Preach with an eye on Christ, depending upon him to grant me the wisdom, grace and power I need as a Christian and as a preacher?

The last question deserves special attention. While evaluating your preaching, you will soon find yourself convicted of many sins. This is humbling and can be terrifying. How dreadful are the words of James 3:1-2a: 'My brethren, be not many masters, knowing that we shall receive the greater condemnation. For in many things we offend all.'[13]

Lest your conscience overwhelm you, you must always evaluate your preaching in the presence of the Lamb who was slain. Depend upon his illumination so that you can rightly evaluate your ministry. Rely upon his atonement to cover your shortcomings. Lean upon his sovereign power to overcome your sins and change you. Evaluate your sermons, not as a condemned sinner who is under law, but as God's child who is under the grace of Christ.

Christ is the only foundation for preaching the Word. He is the foundation of eternal life, the church and Christian ministry. William Perkins said the 'sum of the sum' of his instructions for preachers is, 'Preach one Christ by Christ to the praise of Christ.'[14]

DID I BUILD MY SERMONS WITH THE PRECIOUS MATERIALS OF REFORMED EXPERIENTIAL PREACHING?

Paul says in 1 Corinthians 3:12-13: 'Now if any man build upon this foundation gold, silver, precious stones, wood, hay, stubble; every man's work shall be made manifest: for the day shall declare it, because it shall be revealed by fire; and the fire shall try every man's work of what sort it is.' Earlier, Paul warned us to be careful how we build upon the foundation (v. 10). Now he elaborates this point by telling us what materials we are to use. The contrast between them is not one of strength, like steel versus paper, but of value and beauty, as marble and gold differ from wood and straw; the building under construction is the Lord's glorious temple, not a man's wooden house.[15] The Lord will test our materials by fire on the last day. Fire often symbolizes the presence and glory of the Lord, who dwelled in his temple in a pillar of fire and will come again in fire 'on the day of the Lord'.

Paul speaks here about the day when our Lord Jesus will come with flaming fire to judge each person's works and glorify his saints.[16] These verses have been taken out of context to support the Roman Catholic doctrine of purgatory, which is an imaginary place where fire burns sin out of Christians before they can enter heaven, a place of temporal punishment for sin and purification from sin.[17] But this concept is not found in Scripture and counters the full forgiveness that Christ's finished work grants believers.

Note that this text speaks of testing, not punishment. Materials, not people, are placed in the fire. Within its context, this verse speaks of Christ's judgement of his servants' teaching ministry. Christ will evaluate the materials they used in ministering to the church.

The gold, silver and precious stones, as well as wood, hay and stubble, represent the efforts of preachers such as Paul, Apollos and others. The contrast between gold and hay does not symbolize the difference between gospel and heresy, for Paul says in verse 12 that men 'build upon this foundation', that is, they all preach Christ and not some false gospel.

Rather, the contrast between gold and straw symbolizes God's wisdom versus man's wisdom. Paul begins describing this difference in 1 Corinthians

1:17 and develops it through 1 Corinthians 3. Thus, God's wisdom is the precious treasure by which the preacher builds and adorns God's temple. Paul calls himself a 'wise master-builder' (v. 10), who builds the church by laying its foundation of the gospel of Christ, then adding the gold, silver and precious stones of divine wisdom.[18]

John Gill said that Paul uses the metaphors of wood, hay and stubble to describe, 'not heretical doctrines, damnable heresies, such as are diametrically opposite to, and overturn the foundation ... but empty, trifling, useless things are meant; such as fables, endless genealogies, human traditions, Jewish rites and ceremonies ... the wisdom of the world, the philosophy of the Gentiles'.[19]

Divine wisdom is thus the only acceptable building material that preachers can use. The first two chapters of 1 Corinthians explain that God's wisdom is *biblical*, coming only from words of divine revelation, not from fallen human reasoning (1 Cor. 2:10-13). His wisdom is also *doctrinal*, granting a definite knowledge of God's graces, such as justification and sanctification (1 Cor. 1:30; 2:9-10). This wisdom is Christ-centred (1 Cor. 1:17, 22-24; 2:2), going beyond the foundation of the gospel to build up the church's faith and life. The wisdom of God is *experiential*, granted by the Holy Spirit to work in our inner person to overcome the spirit of the world and create in us the mind of Christ (1 Cor. 2:12, 14-16). And this wisdom is eminently *practical*, for in it we encounter the power of God that changes how we live (1 Cor. 1:18, 24; 2:4, 5; 4:19-20; *cf.* 6:9-11). These are the hallmarks of Reformed experiential preaching, which is biblical, doctrinal, experiential and practical.[20]

So before Christ evaluates your sermons, take time to throw out the straw or stubble in them and replace them with nuggets of gold. A temple worthy of God must be built of the sturdiest, purest and most precious material. Test your sermons by asking: 'Did I build these with the precious materials of Reformed experiential preaching?'

We have already considered questions that evaluate how *biblical* your sermon was. You must also test your sermon to see how *doctrinal* it was. Thomas Murphy wrote:

> *It is taken for granted that the sermon in which there is much doctrine must necessarily be dry, unspiritual, full of sectarianism and almost necessarily incomprehensible... In fact there can be no preaching without doctrine... The attributes of God, the mysteries of the Trinity, the fall of our race, the incarnation, life, death, and ascension of Christ, salvation by his blood, faith, conversion, the Church, the resurrection, judgment, heaven and hell — what are all these but doctrines?[21]*

When asking yourself whether you built your sermons with the precious materials of Reformed experiential preaching with respect to doctrine, ask specifically, did I:

- Approach the Bible to find directions for success, or to listen and learn the truth?
- Refer to the confessions, catechisms and theology of the church?
- Present clear teaching about God that flowed naturally from the biblical text?
- Show how that same doctrine is taught in other parts of the Bible?
- Express the truths of theology in terms that are clear to ordinary believers?
- Help people to understand classic doctrinal terms such as *justification*?
- Connect the doctrine of your Scripture text to related biblical doctrines?
- Base every application upon doctrinal truths drawn from a specific text of Scripture?

In addition, ask yourself how *experiential* your sermon was. Did your sermon communicate to people that Christianity must be experienced, tasted, enjoyed and lived in the power of the Holy Spirit? In its three main divisions, the *Heidelberg Catechism* suggests three dimensions of Christian experience.

DID I BUILD MY SERMONS WITH REFORMED PREACHING?

Ask yourself, did I:

- Speak of the experience of the misery of sin due to its great evil in God's eyes?
- Speak of the experience of deliverance, our glad confidence in Christ's salvation and sufficiency?
- Speak of the experience of gratitude, stirred in our renewed hearts by God's love, to love and obey him?

Experiential preaching is like a sergeant on the battlefield who sets tactical goals, recognizing that war is a mess yet offers hope through strategic victory. Did I:

- Talk about how the Christian life *ought to go* — a lofty ideal for a life-long pursuit?
- Talk about how the Christian life *does go* in reality — encouraging believers in their defeats to look to Christ?
- Talk about how the Christian life *will ultimately go* — pointing them to hope in the final victory in glory?

Experiential preaching also uses the keys of the kingdom to draw lines of demarcation so that each listener can evaluate his spiritual position. Did I:

- Distinguish between the children of God and children of the world?
- Distinguish between Christian experience and the counterfeit graces of hypocrites?
- Distinguish among the different levels of Christian maturity?

Furthermore, you should ask how *practical* your sermon was. Application should not be given like a big bang at the end of the message. Each point of the sermon should be applied. *The Westminster Directory for the Public Worship of God* includes a chapter titled 'Of the Preaching of the Word', which presents several kinds of application. So ask yourself, did I use a variety of applications such as:

- Instruction — to shape the mind and worldview with God's truth?
- Confutation — to expose and refute the doctrinal errors of our day?
- Exhortation — to press God's people to obey God's laws by the means he provides?
- Dehortation — to rebuke sin and stir up hatred for it?
- Comfort — to encourage believers to press forward in the fight of faith?
- Trial — to present the marks of a true believer for self-examination?[22]

- Exultation — to help people see the beauty and glory of God so that they might love him, fear him, and praise him with affection?

God's wisdom is worth more than gold, silver and precious stones. It brings all of life under the counsel of God for our wholehearted happiness. The wisdom of the Scriptures is the only material worthy of use in God's holy temple. Therefore, do not build your sermons with the materials of man which will perish in God's flaming glory. Give your listeners golden words.

DID I PREACH
FOR THE MASTER'S REWARD?

The apostle says in 1 Corinthians 3:14-15: 'If any man's work abide which he hath built thereupon, he shall receive a reward. If any man's work shall be burned, he shall suffer loss: but he himself shall be saved; yet so as by fire.' Though you and your hearers may have long forgotten the specifics of what you preached, the Lord will judge every sermon. Every sermon will have one of two outcomes on Judgement Day: it may be found precious in God's sight and receive his approbation, or it will be judged unworthy and the fire of God's glory will consume it.

What a waste it is to build a sermon, not of the eternal materials of God's wisdom in Christ, but on man's flimsy, cheap wisdom. If you build your sermons in part on your own wisdom, you will lose some of your reward, but not your salvation, for that is built upon the foundation of the gospel of Christ.

Nevertheless, you will forfeit the reward that you might have enjoyed for all eternity. As Gordon Fee writes in his commentary:

> Paul's point is unquestionably warning. It is unfortunately possible for people to attempt to build a church out of every imaginable human system predicated on merely worldly wisdom, be it philosophy, 'pop' psychology, managerial techniques, relational 'good feelings', or what have you. But at the final judgment, all such building … will be shown for what it is: something merely human, with no character of Christ or his gospel in it. [23]

A servant must work for his Master's reward by doing his Master's will. Jesus did not think it wrong to seek a reward but encouraged his disciples to live daily with an eye on the Father's reward (Matt. 6:1-21). We must labour to express our love for God and to please him. The anticipation of Judgement Day should motivate us to evaluate our ministries today out of the glad hope of hearing the Lord say, 'Well done, good and faithful servant!' You cannot undo the errors of the past, but you can find forgiveness with God and grow in faithfulness for the future.

Hoping for the positive evaluation of our Master will release us from catering to the tastes of people. How many sermons have been corrupted by people-pleasing! After denouncing the preacher of a false gospel as under God's curse, Paul asks in Galatians 1:10: 'Do I seek to please men? for if I yet pleased men, I should not be the servant of Christ.' Which master are you trying to please: the harsh slave-master of popular opinion, or the gracious Master who died for your sins? To help find out, ask yourself some more questions about your sermons. Did I:

- Add or subtract anything from my sermon to win the approval of people?
- Preach with the boldness of a clear conscience before God, or in fear of my listeners?
- Preach with a profound sense of reverence, fear and awe of God?
- Preach with gladness that the Lord will honour me if I honour him, or with the frustration of wanting more honour among people?
- Preach ultimately for the pleasure of the audience of One?

Regarding the teaching office of the Old Testament priest, Malachi 2:5-7 says: 'My covenant was with him of life and peace; and I gave them to him for the fear wherewith he feared me, and was afraid before my name. The law of truth was in his mouth, and iniquity was not found in his lips: he walked with me in peace and equity, and did turn many away from iniquity. For the priest's lips should keep knowledge, and they should seek the law at his mouth: for he is the messenger of the Lord of hosts.' Pastors, as messengers of the Lord of hosts, speak with holy fear. Do not be a court jester but a herald of the King.

Preach with your eyes upon Jesus, who is seated at the right hand of God and will come with glory. Remember what Paul says to Timothy, 'I charge thee therefore before God, and the Lord Jesus Christ, who shall judge the quick and the dead at his appearing and his kingdom; preach the word' (2 Tim. 4:1-2).

Preach toward the finish line

Until four, young American skiers went to the 2010 Winter Olympics, the United States had never won a medal in the Nordic Combined event. The Nordic Combined involves individual ski-jumping and cross-country skiing for six miles, and team competition in a ski relay race for twelve miles. The American team won one gold and three silver medals in three Nordic Combined events in those Games.[24] After winning the gold medal, one team member gave a gold ring to his girlfriend, asking her to marry him. She said, 'Yes!'[25] What a way to celebrate!

How much greater will be the joy of the faithful preacher when his Master rewards him in the everlasting kingdom! He will look into the smiling face of the Lord Jesus, the great Bridegroom who loved his church and laid down his life for her. He will receive honour and commendation from the

King of kings. He will look upon the men, women and children whom he served from the pulpit, many of whom will now be clothed with the glory that shines brighter than any earthly gold. Surely that will be worth every drop of energy we put into preaching the Word. If our Lord will reward us for offering a cup of water to people in his name, how much more he will reward us for the hours we spend preparing, preaching and evaluating our sermons.

So evaluate your preaching as a servant anticipating his master's evaluation. Regularly ask yourself these five questions: Did I preach as God's servant? Did I preach to build God's church? Did I preach Christ as the only foundation? Did I build with the precious materials of Reformed experiential preaching? Did I preach for my Master's reward?

Make every effort to grow as a preacher. Eternity will prove it time well spent.

SERMON EVALUATION CHART

[Copy for repeated use]

Evaluate your preaching as a servant anticipating his master's evaluation (1 Cor. 3:5-15).

DID I PREACH AS GOD'S SERVANT?

a. The test of *humble exegesis*. Ask, did I:

- Approach the Scripture with a willingness to be taught and corrected by God, or did I assume that I already knew what the Scripture said?
- Spend enough time and energy to study that Scripture text and let God speak to me through it?
- Read the commentaries of godly and wise teachers to check my interpretation?
- Derive the main idea and points from the clear statement of a Scripture text?
- Spend time explaining what the text meant so my listeners could better understand it?
- Base applications of my sermon on the Scriptures, not just on my vision for the church?
- Preach a message that was faithful to the text's meaning in its context?

- Demonstrate to my hearers that the sermon came from God's Word and not my ideas?

b. The test of *humble dependence*. Did I:

- Plan this series and this specific sermon, prayerfully asking God for wisdom?
- Enlist my congregation to pray for my preaching?
- Study the Scripture text on my knees, with fervent pleas for illumination?
- Prepare the sermon in the context of regular, private prayers for the church?
- Cry out to God prior to the worship services for the Spirit's anointing?
- Cry out to God after the services for divine application?
- Give all the glory to God for any good that resulted from my efforts?

Did I preach to build God's church?

a. The test of *helpfulness*. Ask yourself, did I:

- Write my sermon with an eye to my flock and their needs?
- Labour hard and long on this sermon out of love, or was I lazy?
- Organize the message to make listening easier for people?

- Begin with an introduction to engage their minds and lead them to the main idea?
- Clearly state the main idea of the message?
- Highlight the main points so that listeners recognized them?
- State my main idea and points so succinctly that a twelve-year-old boy and a seventy-year-old woman could write them in their notes?
- Help people understand ancient culture and customs foreign to their world?
- Limit my time and amount of content to what my hearers can absorb profitably?
- Illustrate each major point to engage their imagination and affections?
- Craft my illustrations so as to make them helpful for understanding and applying the gospel?
- Make specific applications throughout the sermon relevant to people's lives?
- Conclude the sermon by pressing the main idea home to my hearers?
- Express the loving heart of the Father who calls the prodigal to come home?
- Call the unsaved to repentance and faith in Christ?

b. The test of *spiritual needs*. Ask, did I:

- Rebuke unbelievers who are ignorant and unteachable?
- Offer basic catechetical truths to unbelievers who are ignorant but teachable?

SERMON EVALUATION CHART

- State the terms of the law to unbelievers with knowledge but who are not yet believers?
- Offer the gospel call of Christ to unbelievers humbled by sin?
- Explain the doctrines of grace and the rule of life to believers?
- Stress the doctrines of repentance and hope to backsliding believers?

c. The test of *love*. Did I preach with affection and kindness to my hearers?

DID I PREACH CHRIST AS THE ONLY FOUNDATION?

a. The test of *the Bread of life*. Ask yourself, did I:

- Write this sermon in the confidence that Christ, in his offices of Prophet, Priest and King, has in himself the fulness of wisdom, grace and power that everyone needs?
- Write this knowing that Christ is Bible's main character and fulfilment of its every theme?
- Connect this text to Christ so that people will be encouraged to lean upon him in trust?
- Thoughtfully consider how this text points to Christ?
- Seek to display men's need for grace and Christ's full provision of grace?
- Press upon hearers their obligation to keep God's law as well as to seek justification before God by

faith alone in Christ alone?

- Direct people to obey by faith in the sanctifying grace of Jesus Christ?
- Explain that the gospel is both for the salvation of the lost and the lives of the saved?
- Preach Christ not only as useful to us but as gloriously beautiful and worthy of our worship?
- Preach with an eye on Christ, depending confidently upon him to grant me the wisdom, grace and power I needed as a Christian and as a preacher?

b. The test of *preaching under grace.* Am I evaluating my preaching trusting in the Lamb who was slain?

Did I build with the precious materials of Reformed experiential preaching?

a. The test of *biblical* preaching (see pp. 38-39)
b. The test of *doctrinal* preaching. Ask, did I:

- Approach the Bible to find directions for success, or to listen and learn the truth?
- Refer to the confessions, catechisms and theology of the church?
- Present clear teaching about God that flowed naturally from the biblical text?
- Show how that same doctrine is taught in other parts of the Bible?

Sermon Evaluation Chart

- Express the truths of theology in terms that are clear to ordinary believers?
- Help people to understand classic doctrinal terminology like *justification*?
- Connect the doctrine of your Scripture text to related biblical doctrines?
- Base every application upon doctrinal truth drawn from a specific text of Scripture?

c. The test of *experiential* preaching
— *the three dimensions of Christian experience* (*Heidelberg Catechism*). Did I:

- Speak of the experience of the misery of sin due to its great evil in God's eyes?
- Speak of the experience of deliverance, our glad confidence in Christ's salvation and sufficiency?
- Speak of the experience of gratitude, stirred in our renewed hearts by God's love, to love and obey him?

— *the battlefield mentality*. Did I:

- Talk about how the Christian life *ought to go* — a lofty ideal for life-long pursuit?
- Talk about how the Christian life *does go* in reality — encouraging believers in their defeats to look to Christ?
- Talk about how the Christian life *will go* ultimately — pointing them to hope in the final victory in glory?

— *the keys of the kingdom.* Did I:

- Distinguish between the children of God and children of the world?
- Distinguish between Christian experience and the counterfeit graces of hypocrites?
- Distinguish among the different levels of Christian maturity?

d. The test of *practical* preaching. Did I use a variety of applications like:

- Instruction — to shape the mind and worldview with God's truth?
- Confutation — to expose and refute the doctrinal errors of our day?
- Exhortation — to press God's people to obey God's laws by the means he provides?
- Dehortation — to rebuke sin and stir up hatred for it?
- Comfort — to encourage believers to press forward in the fight of faith?
- Trial — to present the marks of a true believer for self-examination?
- Exultation — to help people see the beauty and glory of God so that they might love him, fear him, and praise him with affection?

Sermon Evaluation Chart

Did I preach
for my Master's reward?

Did I:

- Add or subtract anything from my sermon in order to win the approval of people?
- Preach with the boldness of a clear conscience before God, or in fear of my listeners?
- Preach with a profound sense of reverence, fear and awe toward God?
- Preach with gladness that the Lord will honour me if I honour him, or with the frustration of wanting more honour among people?
- Preach ultimately for the pleasure of the audience of One?

NOTES

1. http://sportsillustrated.cnn.com/2010/ olympics/2010/writers/alexander_wolff/02/23/ kramer.netherlands/index.html, accessed 11-10-10. I thank Paul Smalley for his assistance on this address which I gave in Homiletics I at Puritan Reformed Theological Seminary, 16 November 2010.

2. C. H. Spurgeon, 'The Necessity of Ministerial Progress', in *Lectures to My Students* (1881; reprint, Pasadena: Pilgrim Publications, 1990), 2.23, 28.

3. Charles Hodge, *A Commentary on 1 & 2 Corinthians* (1857–1859; reprint, Edinburgh: Banner of Truth, 1994), 51.

4. D. Martyn Lloyd-Jones, *Preaching & Preachers* (Grand Rapids: Zondervan, 1971), 305.

5. In each of the three clauses of 1 Cor. 3:9, the word 'God's' (*theou*) is pushed to the beginning. See Gordon D. Fee, *The First Epistle to the Corinthians* (Grand Rapids: Eerdmans, 1987), 134.

6. J. I. Packer, 'Introduction: Why Preach?' in *The Preacher and Preaching: Reviving the Art in the Twentieth Century*,

ed. Samuel T. Logan, Jr (Phillipsburg: Presbyterian & Reformed, 1986), 2.

7. William Perkins, 'The Art of Prophecying', ch. 7, in *The Workes of... William Perkins* (London: John Legatt, 1612–1613), 2.752-56.

8. Thomas Murphy, *Pastoral Theology* (1877; reprint Audubon: Old Paths, 1996), 194.

9. Iain H. Murray, *Jonathan Edwards: A New Biography* (Edinburgh: Banner of Truth, 1987), 162.

10. Murray, *Jonathan Edwards: A New Biography*, 148-49.

11. If the laying of the foundation in this context referred to the person and atoning work of Christ, then only God could be said to have laid the foundation (Isa. 28:6; 1 Peter 2:6). Since Paul laid the foundation then Christ must function as the foundation through to the preaching the gospel of Christ. Hodge, *1 & 2 Corinthians*, 55.

12. Matthew Henry, *Commentary on the Whole Bible: New Modern Edition*, 6 vols. (Peabody, Mass.: Hendrickson, 1991), 6.418.

13. Or as the ESV puts it: 'Not many of you should become teachers, my brothers, for you know that we who teach will be judged with greater strictness. For we all stumble in many ways' (James 3:1-2a).

14. Perkins, *Workes*, 2.762.

15. 'Precious stones here mean stones valuable for building, such as granite and marble. Gold and silver were extensively employed in adoring ancient temples, and are therefore appropriately used as the symbols of pure doctrine. Wood, hay and stubble

are the perishable materials out of which ordinary houses were built, but not temples. Wood for the doors and posts; hay [*chortos*], dried grass mixed with mud for the walls; and straw [*kalame*], for the roof. These materials, unsuitable for the temple of God, are appropriate symbols of false doctrines.' Hodge, *1&2 Corinthians*, 56.

16. Rom. 2:5, 16; 13:12-13; 1 Cor. 1:8; 5:5; 2 Cor. 1:14; Eph. 4:30; Phil. 1:6, 10; 2:16; 1 Thess. 5:2, 5, 8; 2 Thess. 2:2.

17. *The Catechism of the Catholic Church* (Mahwah: Paulist Press, 1994), 268-69, 370-72 [sec. 1030-1032, 1472, 1479].

18. Hodge, *1&2 Corinthians*, 56. Fee, *The First Epistle to the Corinthians*, 136-42.

19. John Gill, *Exposition of the Old and New Testaments*, 9 vols (1809; reprint, Paris, Ark: Baptist Standard Bearer, 1989), 8.617.

20. See 'Applying the Word', in Joel R. Beeke, *Living for God's Glory: An Introduction to Calvinism* (Orlando: Reformation Trust, 2008), 255-74.

21. Murphy, *Pastoral Theology*, 175-76.

22. *The Westminster Directory of Public Worship*, discussed by Mark Dever & Sinclair Ferguson (Ross-Shire: Christian Focus, 2008), 95-96.

23. Fee, *The First Epistle to the Corinthians*, 145.

24. http://vancouver2010.com\olympic-nordic-combined, accessed 11-10-10.

25. http://today.msnbc.msn.com/id/35600802/ns/today-today_in_vancouver, accessed 11-10-10.